Common Bird Songs

Donald J. Borror

Department of Zoology and Entomology,
Ohio State University

DOVER PUBLICATIONS, INC.
Mineola, New York

Bibliographical Note

Common Bird Songs CD and Book is a retitled and reset republication of *Common Bird Songs,* first published by Dover Publications, Inc., in record format in 1967, cassette format in 1984, and CD format in 2003.

The illustrations in this booklet have been taken from the following sources: Witmer Stone, *Bird Studies at Old Cape May,* 2 vols., Delaware Valley Ornithological Club, 1937 (reprinted by Dover Publications, 1965), illustrated by Earle L. Poole and Conrad Roland; George Miksch Sutton, *An Introduction to the Birds of Pennsylvania,* J. Horace McFarland Company, 1928, illustrated by the author. The illustrations of the House Sparrow, Baltimore Oriole, and Summer Tanager were prepared specially for this publication by Norman Dreyer.

International Standard Book Number (CD edition): 0-486-99609-3

Manufactured in the United States of America
Dover Publications, Inc., 31 East 2nd Street, Mineola, N.Y. 11501

CONTENTS

INTRODUCTION

This CD is designed primarily for people who want to learn to recognize birds by their songs. It is impossible in a single CD to include all the songs of all the birds one might hear in the United States, but the songs on the CD are of relatively common and widely distributed species, and they should give the listener some idea of the variety of bird songs and calls, and the things about them to note in order to recognize them. Although all of the songs were recorded in the eastern United States, many of the birds are also found in the West.

Of the birds heard here, the following species are on the Audubon WatchList: Cerulean Warbler, Blue-winged Warbler, Kentucky Warbler, Prairie Warbler, Willow Flycatcher, and Wood Thrush. These are species that are already recognized as needing our help because their populations are decreasing to a dangerous degree. Only by careful monitoring and habitat protection can we conserve these declining populations and prevent more of these species from joining the WatchList. Let's keep our common birds common!

Since the 1960s, when these recordings were made, the names of some birds have changed somewhat. Current names are given in footnotes.

There are many instances among birds in which two or more species have very similar songs; the way to learn such songs is to learn the songs of one of these species well, and then learn the ways the others differ from this one. For this reason, the songs on the CD are arranged more or less according to their general character, beginning with very simple songs and progressing to more complex ones. Similar songs are grouped together so that they can be more readily compared.

The selections for this CD were made from a collection of several thousand recordings, based principally on how typical each was for the species concerned. Songs of two or more individuals are included in many cases, to show something of the variation in the species; each "example" is from a different bird, and on the CD the different examples are generally designated by numbers.

Bird vocalizations are sometimes roughly classified into two groups, songs and calls. The distinction between these two groups is not easily drawn, but a bird's songs are generally more complex than its calls, they are heard principally (or solely) in the spring and summer, and they are usually uttered only by the male. Songs serve to advertise the presence of the male, to attract a female, and/or to repel other males of the same species from the singer's territory. Vocalizations that are calls rather than songs are included for some of the species; because they are frequently heard and are fairly distinctive.

The intraspecific variation in bird songs often presents a problem for the person trying to learn to recognize birds by their song. In many species the songs of a given individual are essentially alike, but the songs of different individuals may differ; in other species each individual may sing two or more different songs. Examples of both of these types of variation are included on the CD. One learns to recognize species of birds by their songs not only on the basis of the particular song or song pattern they sing, but by the *kind* of song they sing, and by the general quality of the song.

In the following accounts of the species on the CD no attempt is made to describe each bird or to indicate its geographic range. This information is available in various bird guides, and the listener might profitably have such a guide at hand when listening to the CD.

The following accounts contain brief descriptions of each species' song, and contain frequent references to particular songs on the CD (usually by its number in a series); it is suggested that the listener refer to these accounts when listening to the CD.

It is very difficult to make a recording of a bird in the field without getting the sounds of other birds in the background. Background songs are generally inconspicuous in the recordings on the CD, but in many cases they are loud enough to be recognizable. They are neither mentioned nor identified in the following accounts, and thus may be used to test the listener's knowledge of bird songs; most of these background birds are featured elsewhere on the CD.

One characteristic of a bird's singing, which is sometimes useful in distinguishing species with similar songs, is not always accurately reproduced in the CD; this is the interval between successive songs. Many of our common birds sing short songs, a couple of seconds in length, at the rate of three to six a minute, and to include all this silent interval would result in a lot of unused space on the CD. In many cases where two or more songs from a single recording are used, a portion of the interval between songs has been cut out in order to get more songs on the CD. The bird's normal singing rate is frequently mentioned in the following accounts, and is *always* mentioned when it is markedly different from the rate on the CD.

The songs and calls in this track are relatively simple, and many can be paraphrased with words or phrases. Each usually consists of a single note or phrase, which may be repeated fairly rapidly or at irregular intervals. The calls of the first four species in this track are harsh, nasal, or relatively unmusical; the calls of the remaining species are clear whistles, which can be imitated by a good whistler.

COMMON CROW
Corvus brachyrhynchos

The calls of the **Common Crow*** are well known, and are usually described as a *caw* or *cah*. The quality of these calls and the rate at which they are uttered are subject to quite a bit of variation. In Example 1 a single bird is calling at intervals of several seconds; in Example 2 a group of crows is calling in response to the presence nearby of a Great Horned Owl.

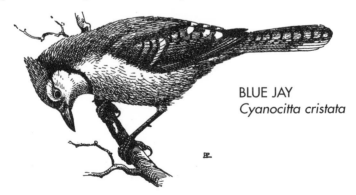

BLUE JAY
Cyanocitta cristata

The **Blue Jay** utters a great variety of calls, but one of the most common is a harsh nasal note, heard in Example 1; this is a scolding call. The sounds which appear to be songs are in the nature of squeaky whistles, usually uttered in groups of two or three; Examples 2 and 3 contain songs.

---

*American Crow.

COMMON NIGHTHAWK
Chordeiles minor

The call of the **Common Nighthawk** is a loud nasal *peeah,* which is uttered as the bird flies about.

HOUSE SPARROW
Passer domesticus

The **House Sparrow** (formerly called the **English Sparrow**), one of the most common birds in cities and around farm buildings, utters a variety of chattering or chirping calls. The bird on the CD is a male; the calls of the female are a little different.

The last three species in Track 1 have short whistled calls, and in the case of the Bobwhite and Whip-poor-will the name of the bird is derived from a paraphrasing of the call. The common call of the **Bobwhite*** is a loud clear *bob bob white*, but the first *bob* is often quite weak; occasionally (call 4) the first *bob* is omitted.

BOBWHITE
Colinus virginianus

RED-SHOULDERED HAWK
Buteo lineatus

The common call of the **Red-shouldered Hawk** is a loud, piercing, down-slurred whistle; it may be uttered from a perch

---

*Northern Bobwhite.

or on the wing. The **Whip-poor-will** is one of the few birds that call only at night, and the calls are often uttered regularly for long periods; the *poor* of the *whip-poor-will* call is somewhat wavering.

WHIP-POOR-WILL
Caprimulgus vociferus

The songs and calls in this track are short and relatively simple, and many can be easily paraphrased.

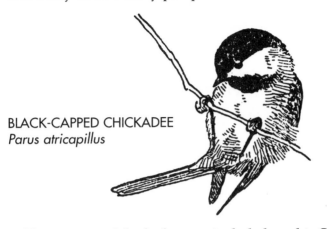

BLACK-CAPPED CHICKADEE
Parus atricapillus

Two species of chickadees are included on this CD, the Black-capped Chickadee and the Carolina Chickadee. The two species are very similar in appearance, but have different songs and calls. The song of the **Black-capped Chickadee** usually consists of three clear whistled notes, each steady in pitch; the second and third are in the same pitch, a little lower than the first, and somewhat run together. The song of the **Carolina Chickadee** usually consists of four clear whistled notes, the second lower than the first, the third a little higher than the second but not as high as the first, and the fourth lower than the second; the first and third notes are often very short. Songs of this species which end after the second note (and some of them do) can be distinguished from the songs of the Black-capped Chickadee by the greater drop in pitch from the first note to the second.

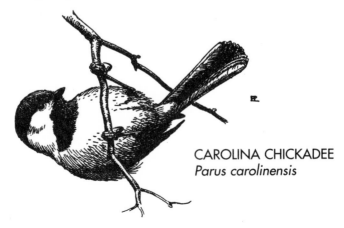

CAROLINA CHICKADEE
Parus carolinensis

Both species of chickadees have a number of calls, but one of the most characteristic is a *chick-a-dee-dee-dee,* from which the bird gets its name. These calls are very similar in the two species, but the *dees* are generally faster in the Carolina Chickadee than in the Black-capped.

EASTERN WOOD PEWEE
Contopus virens

The usual singing of the **Eastern Wood Pewee** includes two slightly different songs, a clear plaintive *pee-ah-wee,* and a *peee-ah.* These two types of songs are sung more or less alternately, but the bird usually sings about three times as many *pee-ah-wees* as *peee-ahs.* Songs 2 and 6 are *peee-ah* songs; the others are *pee-ah-wee* songs.

EASTERN PHOEBE
Sayornis phoebe

The **Eastern Phoebe** also has two slightly different songs which it sings more or less alternately. Each might be paraphrased *fee-bee,* but one ends in a buzz and the other ends in a sputter. Songs 3, 5, 7, 9, and 11 end in a sputter; the others end in a buzz.

LEAST FLYCATCHER
Empidonax minimus

The call of the **Least Flycatcher** is a sharp *che-bec;* these calls are usually uttered in rapid succession.

GREAT CRESTED FLYCATCHER
Myiarchus crinitus

The **Great Crested Flycatcher** utters a variety of clear whistled notes and loud trills. The most common whistled note is a loud *wheep,* heard in Example 1; trills and a few short whistles are heard in Example 2.

The **Traill's Flycatcher*** has a short, somewhat sneezy song that varies slightly in different parts of the country. The southern birds' song is usually paraphrased as *fitz-bew,* but these birds actually have three slightly different songs: a short *fisst* (song 2 in Example 1), a *fitz-bew* (songs 1, 4, and 5 in Example 1), and a *fizz-bew* (song 3 in Example 1); these three types are sung more or less alternately, but not in any fixed sequence. The *fisst* is easily distinguished from the other two, but it takes a sharp ear to distinguish the *fitz-bew* from the *fizz-bew.* The northern birds (Example 2), which may really be a different species, have a single song that might be described as a *fee-bee-o,* with the *fee* slightly stuttering.

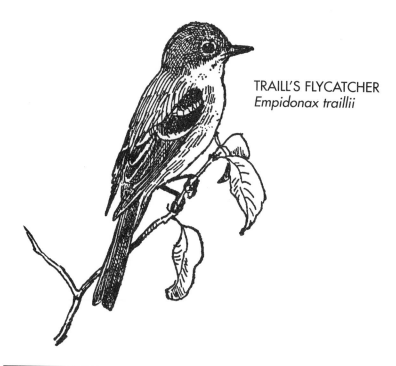

TRAILL'S FLYCATCHER
Empidonax traillii

---

*Traill's Flycatcher has been split into the Willow Flycatcher *(Empidonax traillii)* and the Alder Flycatcher *(Empidonax alnorum).* The Alder Flycatcher is more northern, but the ranges overlap. The two are very difficult to separate by sight, but have different vocalizations. Example 1 on the CD is the Willow Flycatcher (the "southern birds" referred to above); Example 2 (the "northern birds") is the Alder Flycatcher.

The songs of the first two species in this track consist of a rapid series of similar notes, usually uttered slowly enough to be counted; the songs of the last four species consist of a rapid series of similar notes or phrases generally uttered too fast to be counted, producing what might be called a trill.

WHITE-BREASTED NUTHATCH
Sitta carolinensis

The **White-breasted Nuthatch** utters a series of nasal notes. When the bird is feeding (Example 1) these notes are uttered irregularly; the song (Example 2) consists of a fairly rapid series of several nasal notes. The song sounds a little like the song of a flicker that is some distance away, but is more nasal in quality and shorter.

The **Yellow-shafted Flicker*** utters a long series of short whistled notes: *wick-wick-wick-wick-wick-;* the last few *wicks* are sometimes a little weaker or lower in pitch than the rest. These series are uttered at the rate of 3 or 4 a minute.

---

*Northern Flicker.

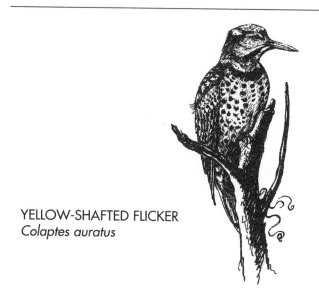

YELLOW-SHAFTED FLICKER
Colaptes auratus

CHIPPING SPARROW
Spizella passerina

Chipping Sparrow songs are trills—rapid series of similar notes or phrases usually uttered too fast to be counted—having a rather dull or mechanical quality; most songs are 2 or 3 seconds in length. The songs of a given bird may vary in length; those of different birds often vary in the character of the individual notes or phrases and the rate with which they are uttered. The phrases usually sound 1-noted, but sometimes actually contain 2 (Examples 2 and 5) or 3 (Example 1) notes. The songs on the CD are arranged in an order of increasing phrase rate, from 7.4 phrases per second in Example 1 to 15.9 per second in Example 8.

The songs of the **Slate-colored Junco*** are very similar to those of the Chipping Sparrow, but average a little shorter (1 or 2 seconds in length), and are a little more musical, or tinkling, in quality. The individual phrases contain from 2 to 5 notes

---

*Dark-eyed Junco.

SLATE-COLORED JUNCO
Junco hyemalis

each, but usually sound 1- or 2-noted. The songs of a given bird may vary in length; those of different birds often vary in the character of the individual phrases and in the rate at which they are uttered. The songs on the CD are arranged in an order of increasing phrase rate, from 7.2 phrases per second in the first example to 17.7 per second in the last.

SWAMP SPARROW
Melospiza georgiana

The songs of the **Swamp Sparrow** are similar to those of a Chipping Sparrow, but are usually slower (the phrase rate varies from about 5 to 9 per second), and the song has a staccato quality. The individual phrases usually sound 2-noted, but generally contain 3 or 4 notes. The songs of a given bird are usually all of the same pattern (phrase type); the songs of different birds may differ in the character of the individual phrases and the rate at which they are uttered. The songs on the CD are arranged in an order of increasing phrase rate, from 5.1 per second in the first example to 9.1 per second in the last.

NASHVILLE WARBLER
Vermivora ruficapilla

The songs of the **Nashville Warbler** are usually a 2-parted trill, with the second part faster and lower in pitch. The phrases in the first part usually sound 2-noted, and are uttered at the rate of 4 or 5 per second (slowly enough to be counted); the phrases in the second part are 1-noted, and are uttered at the rate of 6 to 13 per second (usually too fast to be counted). The songs of a given bird contain the same phrase types but may vary in length; the songs of different birds frequently differ in the character and rate of the two types of trill phrases.

The songs in this track consist of a series of similar phrases, but the phrases are uttered slowly enough to be counted and obviously contain more than one note each. It is usually possible to paraphrase these songs with words or phrases.

YELLOWTHROAT
Geothlypis trichas

Songs of the **Yellowthroat** consist of 2 to 5 similar phrases, and each phrase contains from 2 to 5 notes; some songs may start and/or end in the middle of a phrase. The songs of a given bird vary in length; those of different birds often differ in the character of the phrases. The 3-noted phrases of the first four Examples on the CD might be paraphrased *which is it;* the accent in the first, third, and fourth Examples is on the *which,* but in the second Example is on the *is.* Examples 5 and 6 contain 4-note phrases; Example 5 might also be paraphrased *which is it,* but the *which* represents two very rapidly uttered notes; the phrases of Example 6 are more obviously 4-noted. The phrases in the last two Examples are 5-noted.

CAROLINA WREN
Thryothorus ludovicianus

The songs of the **Carolina Wren** are similar to those of the Yellowthroat in consisting of a series of similar phrases, but they usually contain more phrases (up to 8 in northern birds and 12 in southern birds), and the phrases are usually uttered more rapidly. Some songs start and/or end in the middle of a phrase. Each bird has a repertoire of a number of different phrases (or song patterns); it usually sings songs of one pattern for a while, then changes to songs of another pattern. Different birds usually have slightly different song patterns. A Carolina Wren usually sings at the rate of 8 to 12 songs a minute; a Yellowthroat usually sings 5 or 6 songs a minute.

OVENBIRD
Seiurus aurocapillus

The songs of the **Ovenbird** consist of 6 to 12 similar phrases that usually get louder toward the end of the song. The phrases generally sound 2-noted–*p-chee, p-chee*–with the first weak and high-pitched and the second louder and lower in pitch. The songs of a given bird are similar in pattern (or phrase type); those of different birds often differ in pattern, but the differences are generally slight. An Ovenbird usually sings at the rate of 3 or 4 songs a minute.

KENTUCKY WARBLER
Oporornis formosus

The songs of the **Kentucky Warbler** are similar to those of the Ovenbird, but are usually shorter; the different notes in each phrase are about equal in pitch and loudness, or the final note may be a little higher in pitch. The phrases appear a little more rollicking than those of the Ovenbird, and do not get noticeably louder toward the end of the song. Most phrases appear to contain more than two notes. The songs of a given bird are of the same pattern (phrase type), but those of different birds occasionally differ in pattern. A Kentucky Warbler usually sings at the rate of 3 or 4 songs a minute.

The songs in this track consist of clear whistled notes, and many can be imitated by a good whistler. The songs of different species in the group differ in the rhythm and pitch of the songs, and in the character of the individual notes.

FIELD SPARROW
Spizella pusilla

The songs of the **Field Sparrow** consist of a series of clear whistled notes, usually all about the same pitch; the introductory notes are longer and uttered slowly, while the final notes are shorter and uttered more rapidly; the song usually ends in a trill. The transition from the slow introductory notes to the fast final notes may be abrupt or gradual. The introductory notes may be steady in pitch (Example 3), slightly up-slurred (Examples 1 and 4), or slightly down-slurred (Examples 2, 5, and 6). In some songs the pitch rises or falls slightly toward the end of the song. A few songs (e.g., the last on the CD) appear 3-parted, with the note rate faster in the successive parts. The songs of a given bird are usually all alike but may vary in length; some birds may sing songs of two or three slightly different patterns. The songs of different birds often differ slightly. Field Sparrows usually sing at the rate of 4 or 5 songs a minute.

The song of the **White-throated Sparrow** consists of a series of clear whistled notes which are generally steady in pitch or nearly so; occasionally one note in the song may be abruptly slurred at

WHITE-THROATED SPARROW
Zonotrichia albicollis

the beginning. The song generally ends in a series of 3-parted notes, or triplets. There is nearly always at least one pitch change in the song, usually after the first or second note, and some songs contain two or three changes in pitch. A number of different song patterns are sung by these species, each characterized by certain changes in pitch through the song; most birds sing songs of a single pattern (which may vary in length), but a very few may sing songs of two different patterns more or less alternately. The most common song pattern in this species (Examples 1 and 2) consists of a long note, a triplet at a slightly higher pitch, a note a little shorter than the first with an abrupt initial up-slur, and one or more final triplets; the third and remaining notes may be at the same pitch (Example 1), or the final triplets may be slightly lower in pitch (Example 2). This song might be paraphrased *toooo tititi twee tititi tititi tititi,* and it may be heard throughout the species' range. Example 3 is of a pattern confined to the eastern part of the country, and is sung by about one-fourth or more of the birds in New England; it is similar to the pattern of Examples 1 and 2, but the second note is usually 2-parted and is followed by a very short lower note, and the fourth note lacks the initial abrupt up-slur: *toooo teetee p-teee tititi tititi tititi.* The pattern of Example 4, which is less common but occurs throughout the species' range, is similar to the patterns of the first three songs but is higher in pitch, and has the third note slightly lower in pitch than the second. Example 5 represents a pattern that is very rare in the East but is relatively common in the Midwest; the first two notes are high-pitched, with the third and remaining notes at a lower pitch: *teee teee tooo tototo tototo tototo.* The last song represents a rather unusual pattern in which the pitch rises through the first four notes, with the fourth note about an octave higher than the first, and with the fifth and remaining notes about the same pitch as the fourth: *tyoo tititi twee tititi teee tititi.*

CARDINAL
Richmondena cardinalis

Cardinal* songs consist of a series of 1 to 30 or more loud, clear, whistled phrases uttered 1 to 9 per second; the first phrase or two are often uttered a little more slowly than the following phrases. The phrases contain 1 to 3 (rarely more) notes, most of which are slurred, some very abruptly. The phrases in a given song may be all alike (Examples 1–4), or the song may contain 2 or 3 (rarely 4 or 5) groups of different phrases. Each bird has a vocabulary of several different phrases, which are used to produce a number of different song patterns; different birds usually have slightly different phrases in their vocabulary. Many songs are relatively easy to paraphrase: *wit-wit-wit-wit* (Example 1), *wherr-ti wherr-ti wherr-ti* (Example 2), *tee-a-to, tee-a-to, tee-a-to* (Example 3), and so on. A Cardinal usually sings at the rate of 5 to 8 songs a minute–songs of one pattern for several songs, then songs of another pattern.

TUFTED TITMOUSE
Parus bicolor

*Northern Cardinal.

28

The songs of the **Tufted Titmouse** are similar to those of a Cardinal, but are usually shorter (with 1 to 7 or 8 phrases), and the phrases usually appear 2-noted. Each bird usually has a vocabulary of 3 or 4 song patterns (phrase types), but sings songs of a given pattern a long time before changing, and many birds may appear to have only a single song pattern. The songs of different birds are often a little different. Tufted Titmouse songs are generally easily paraphrased: *areet areet areet* (Example 1), *fee-be fee-be fee-be* (Example 2), *teeup teeup teeup teeup* (Example 3), and so on. The songs are usually sung at the rate of 10 or 12 a minute.

The songs of the last two species in this track consist of loud whistled notes, but most of the notes are slurred and the songs seldom contain a series of similar notes or phrases.

EASTERN MEADOWLARK
Sturnella magna

The songs of the **Eastern Meadowlark** consist of a series of 3 to 8 or more loud, clear, whistled notes; most notes are down-slurred, but in some songs the introductory note (or notes) is steady in pitch. The pitch trend through the song is usually upward and then downward, with the pitch highest near the middle of the song and dropping toward the end. Many of the slurred notes appear 2- or 3-parted. Each bird has a repertoire of 3 or more different song patterns, and generally sings one pattern for a while before changing to another; the patterns of different birds are usually a little different. The most common call notes are a buzzy *cheeup* (calls 1 and 2 in Example 5), and the *cheeup* followed by a sputtery trill (the remaining calls in Example 5).

29

BALTIMORE ORIOLE
Icterus galbula

Baltimore Oriole songs consist principally of a series of loud, clear, whistled notes; the notes are usually slurred, and some notes may be uttered two or more times in succession in a song. Some songs contain one or more harsh notes. The songs of a given bird are usually very similar but may vary in length; those of different birds often differ considerably. Many birds utter single whistles or 2-note phrases between their longer songs.

The songs in this track are buzzy in quality. A buzzy quality is produced when a bird utters a given note or phrase very rapidly (30 or more times per second), or when a note is fluctuated up and down in pitch 30 or more times a second.

GRASSHOPPER SPARROW
Ammodramus savannarum

Grasshopper Sparrow songs are very high-pitched, and some people may have trouble hearing them. They generally consist of 3 or 4 short notes followed by a long buzz, with a short, high-pitched note at the end. The introductory notes are of a decreasing pitch; when there are four introductory notes (songs 1 and 2 in Example 1) the first, second, and fourth are of decreasing pitch, with the third very weak and high-pitched; most people are unable to hear this third note. The buzz is about 1 to 1½ seconds in length, with the first 0.10 or 0.15 second of it a little louder and lower in pitch than the rest. The songs of the same or different birds are very similar, and often indistinguishable by ear; they may vary in the number of introductory notes, or (in different birds) in the detailed character of the buzz.

BLUE-WINGED WARBLER
Vermivora pinus

Most songs of the **Blue-winged Warbler** consist of two buzzes: *beee bzzzz*. The first buzz usually sounds a little higher in pitch than the second. The songs of the same or different birds are very similar, and are seldom distinguishable by ear.

BLACK-THROATED GREEN WARBLER
Dendroica virens

The songs of the **Black-throated Green Warbler** consist of a series of buzzy or lisping notes, usually on 2 or 3 different pitches. There are two common song patterns in the species, *zeee zeee zoo zoo zee* (Example 1), and *zee zee zee zee zoo zee* (Examples 2 and 3). The songs of the first pattern are very similar in different birds, differing chiefly in the length of the final note; those of the second pattern may differ in the number and rate of the introductory notes.

PRAIRIE WARBLER
Dendroica discolor

The songs of the **Prairie Warbler** consist of a series of short buzzy notes that rise in pitch through the series. The songs of a given bird are similar in note rate, but may vary in length; those of different birds often differ in the length and rate of the notes. Individual songs may contain from 6 to 30 or more notes. The songs are usually sung at the rate of 3 or 4 a minute.

PARULA WARBLER
Parula americana

The songs of the **Parula Warbler** are buzzy in quality, with the last part a little higher in pitch, and they generally end with a short, sharp note. A number of different song patterns occur in this species, but they are of two general types; one type (Example 1) consists of a buzzy trill that rises gradually in pitch and ends in a sharp note; the other type contains longer notes (Examples 2–4). Songs of the first type are very distinctive, and unlike the songs of any other eastern bird; songs of the second type are often very similar to those of the Cerulean Warbler, but differ in having a sharp note at the end. The songs of a given bird are usually all of the same pattern, at least in a single period of singing; on different occasions a bird may sing songs of different patterns.

CERULEAN WARBLER
Dendroica cerulea

The songs of the **Cerulean Warbler** are very similar to the songs of the second type described above for the Parula

Warbler; they consist of a series of buzzy phrases at about the same tempo and pitch, followed by a series of faster phrases and/or a buzz at a higher pitch. The second or higher-pitched part of the song is sometimes (Examples 3, 4, and 6) a single buzz, sometimes (Examples 5 and 7) a series of buzzy notes and a final buzz, sometimes (Examples 1 and 2) rather intermediate in character. Each bird may sing songs of 2 or 3 slightly different patterns, but generally its songs are all of the same pattern; the songs of different birds are often slightly different.

The first species on this track is a Robin, and the next four have songs very similar to those of a Robin. The phrases are short, and contain slurred whistles uttered in rapid succession to produce what might be called a warble. Some species in this group (the Robin, Rose-breasted Grosbeak, and Red-eyed Vireo) have long-continued songs; the two tanagers have short songs separated by a longer silent interval.

ROBIN
Turdus migratorius

Robin* song is long-continued, and consists of loud, clear, whistled phrases. A Robin has a vocabulary of several phrases, and it sings one phrase a time or two, then another phrase a time or two, and then perhaps the first phrase again. Every once in a while there is a chirp or two between phrases, and the final phrase in many series is high-pitched and buzzy. The pauses between phrases vary in length, but the bird usually utters a long series of phrases without any prolonged pauses.

ROSE-BREASTED GROSBEAK
Pheucticus ludovicianus

---

*American Robin.

The song of the **Rose-breasted Grosbeak** is relatively long-continued, like that of a Robin, but there is less distinct phrasing of the notes; the notes are a little more run together. Most note sequences contain about 15 or 20 phrases, with pauses of varying length between sequences. The song has a slightly different quality from that of a Robin, and the individual notes are usually slurred over a greater pitch range. Many birds utter a short sharp *kink* between the phrase sequences; this note is heard at the end of Example 3.

SUMMER TANAGER
Piranga rubra

Summer Tanager song is similar to that of the Robin in quality, but the phrases are a little more bouncy in character, and the song is not long-continued. Each song lasts about 2 seconds, and the bird generally sings 6 to 8 songs a minute.

SCARLET TANAGER
Piranga olivacea

Scarlet Tanager songs are short, not long-continued like those of the Robin, and are a little more hoarse; they sound a little like a Robin with a cold, and are usually a little faster. The songs are sung at the rate of 6 to 8 a minute.

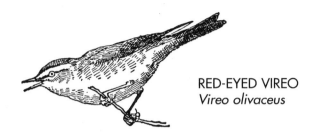

RED-EYED VIREO
Vireo olivaceus

The song of the **Red-eyed Vireo** is long-continued, like that of the Robin, but the phrases are shorter and more separated. This bird is a very persistent singer, and the phrases often continue for several minutes with little or no interruption.

The songs of the last two species in this track might be described as a warble—a fairly rapid series of slurred whistles with very short pauses between notes, so that the notes often appear to be run together.

WARBLING VIREO
Vireo gilvus

The songs of the **Warbling Vireo** consist of 8 to 20 or more slurred whistles, and usually end abruptly on a relatively high note; the bird usually sings 6 to 8 songs a minute.

PURPLE FINCH
Carpodacus purpureus

The songs of the **Purple Finch** are very similar to those of the Warbling Vireo, but they are usually a little louder, they are somewhat less regular in tempo, and they do not ordinarily end on a high note. The songs are generally about 1½ to 2 seconds in length and are sung at the rate of 6 to 8 a minute; sometimes, particularly early in the season, a song may be several seconds in length, or the bird may sing almost continuously.

37

The songs in this track are rather complex, and do not readily fit into any of the song types so far treated.

WOOD THRUSH
Hylocichla mustelina

The songs of the **Wood Thrush** are 1½ to 2 seconds in length, and are generally sung at the rate of 10 to 15 a minute. They are usually 3-parted; the first part consists of 1 to 4 (usually 2 or 3) low, weak, buzzy notes, which may not be heard unless the bird is quite close; the second part is the loudest and most distinctive part of the song, and consists of 2 to 10 or 12 notes which are quite musical in character, and the pitch changes in this part follow our musical scale; the third part is a rapid series of notes that are usually quite high-pitched and buzzy. Each bird has a vocabulary of two or more variations of each part of the song, and these are combined to produce a number of different song patterns; the bird's different patterns are not sung in any fixed sequence, but successive songs are usually different. The songs in Example 1 were sung by a bird that had two variations of the first part of the song, five of the second part, and nine of the third part; most of these part types are included in the songs on the CD. The songs of different birds are nearly always different, although 1 or 2 parts of the songs of different birds are sometimes identical.

The songs of the **Rufous-sided Towhee*** consist of 1 or 2 (rarely 3 or 4) introductory notes followed by a trill; the trill is a series of up to 18 similar phrases, but in some songs (e.g., Examples 5 and 7) it begins with a note or phrase that is different from the remaining trill phrases. The notes in the introduction may be clear whistles or buzzy (or both), and may be

---

*Eastern Towhee.

RUFOUS-SIDED TOWHEE
Pipilo erythrophthalmus

steady in pitch or slurred. Examples 1 and 2 begin with a single note; the introductory note in Example 2 is like the common call of this species, usually described as *ta-wee,* from which the bird gets its name. Most songs (Examples 3–6) begin with 2 notes, which are usually different in pitch; such songs might be paraphrased *drink-your-teeee,* with the *drink* higher in pitch than the *your* (Examples 3–5) or lower (Example 6). Example 7 begins with 3 notes, the first two of which are identical, and Example 8 begins with 4 notes. Each bird usually has a vocabulary of 2 or 3 different introductions and as many different trills, which it combines to produce 3 or 4 (rarely more) different song patterns; a bird usually sings songs of one pattern for a while and then changes to another, but occasionally a bird will sing two song patterns alternately. The songs of different birds are usually a little different.

RED-WINGED BLACKBIRD
Agelaius phoeniceus

Red-winged Blackbird songs consist of 1 to 4 short, low-pitched, often somewhat gurgly notes, followed by a buzz or buzzy trill; most songs end in a short low-pitched note. A common song pattern (Example 1) might be paraphrased *congareeee-a*. In rare cases (e.g., the last Example) the buzzy trill is 2-parted. Each bird has a repertoire of 3 or 4 different song patterns; it usually sings a few songs of one pattern before changing to another. The songs of different birds are often slightly different.

SONG SPARROW
Melospiza melodia

Songs of the **Song Sparrow** are extremely variable; they consist of a series of phrases most of which contain 1 to 4 notes, and they usually contain a trill (a series of up to a dozen or so similar phrases uttered too fast to be counted). Some notes are clear whistles, while some are buzzy; most notes are steady in pitch. Most notes are 0.15 second in length or less, but some of the buzzy notes may be longer (up to ½ second or more). The longer phrases in the song–the ones uttered slowly enough to be counted–are usually single, but sometimes are repeated 2 or 3 times. Most songs (Examples 1–6) begin with 2 to 4 (usually 3) similar phrases uttered at a constant rate; some (Examples 7–9) begin with a series of 4 to 20 similar phrases which increase in rate through the series. Each bird has a vocabulary of a great many different notes and phrases, which are combined to produce up to 10 or 12 quite different song patterns. A bird usually sings about 5 to 7 songs a minute; it normally sings one pattern for a while, then changes to another. The different songs of a given pattern may vary in length, or in the number of notes in different parts of the song. The songs of the birds in a given area usually contain identical phrases, but it is very unusual to find two birds singing identical songs; the songs of birds in different areas usually contain different phrases.

HOODED WARBLER
Wilsonia citrina

The songs of the **Hooded Warbler** are short, loud, and emphatic; the most common pattern (Examples 1–3) might be paraphrased *tawee tawee tawee-tee-to,* with the *tee* high-pitched and accented. Other song patterns (e.g., Example 4) are similar in quality but a little different in phrasing. The songs of a given bird are all of the same pattern but may vary in the number of introductory notes; the songs of different birds are occasionally a little different.

YELLOW WARBLER
Dendroica petechia aestiva

Yellow Warbler songs are of two general types, one (Examples 1–4) a short and characteristically phrased song: *sweet sweet sweet sweeter-than-sweet,* and the other (Examples 5–7) a song of variable length and phrasing. A given bird may sing both types of songs, but during the nesting season most of its songs are of just one type. Songs of the first type consist of two series of down-slurred notes, the first a little slower and higher pitched than the second, and the song ends in a short up-slurred note. The songs of this type are subject to variation in the number of notes they contain, and (in different birds) in the rate and character of the notes. Songs of the second type consist of a series of slurred or wavering notes, usually a few of one type, then a few of another, and so on; successive songs of this type sung by a given bird may be all alike, or (especially early in the season) may represent slightly different patterns.

CHESTNUT-SIDED WARBLER
Dendroica pensylvanica

The songs of the **Chestnut-sided Warbler** are of two general types; one (Examples 1–3) ends in a *meet-ya* phrase, and the other (Examples 4–7) is of variable length and phrasing. Some songs of the first type (Examples 1 and 2) might be paraphrased *very very very very pleased to-meet-ya;* others are similar but end in *meet-meet-ya* (Example 3). Songs of the second type are very similar to the second type songs of the Yellow Warbler, and are sometimes quite difficult to distinguish from them. The songs of a given bird are usually all of the same type, but those of different birds are often a little different.

Songs of the **White-eyed Vireo** are short and emphatic, and although they are subject to a great deal of variation they are usually quite distinctive. Most songs begin and end with a sharp *chick,* and at least 1 or 2 of the notes between the *chicks* are slurred and buzzy, relatively long, and strongly emphasized. Example 1 might be paraphrased *chick weeeer t-dalo chick,* with the *weeeer* long and strongly emphasized, and the *t-dalo* a group of rapidly uttered notes; most songs contain a note similar to this *weeeer,* and practically all songs contain one or two groups of rapidly uttered notes. A few songs may lack the final *chick,* or have it quite weak. Each bird usually has a repertoire of four or five different patterns, and the songs of different birds are usually a little different. A White-eyed Vireo usually sings at the rate of 10 to 15 songs a minute; it sings one pattern for a while, then changes to another.

WHITE-EYED VIREO
Vireo griseus

The songs in this track are rather complex, but most of them contain two or more series of similar phrases, and some are trilly or canary-like in character.

LOUISIANA WATERTHRUSH
Seiurus motacilla

The songs of the **Louisiana Waterthrush*** begin with a series of two or three loud, clear, slurred, whistled notes, and end in a rapid series of short, weak notes. The general effect is of a bird starting out strong but weakening toward the end of the song. The introductory notes are usually of decreasing pitch. The songs of a given bird are usually alike except in length; those of different birds may also differ in the character of the notes they contain.

INDIGO BUNTING
Passerina cyanea

The songs of the **Indigo Bunting** are loud, and consist of a series of phrases about half of which are in twos; the phrases are generally uttered slowly enough to be counted. Most songs contain about 10 or 12 phrases. A typical song (Example 1) might

---

*Waterthrush.

44

be paraphrased *tee-tyu-tyu-chew-chew-tee-tee-wee-wee* (song 2, Example 1, from the same bird, is the same but with an added *chew* on the end). Songs of a given bird usually vary in length, and sometimes also in the particular sequence of the phrases they contain; the phrases of different birds are usually a little different.

VESPER SPARROW
Pooecetes gramineus

    The songs of the **Vesper Sparrow** are somewhat similar to those of an Indigo Bunting, but there are usually more than two similar phrases in a sequence, and the phrases are uttered more rapidly, producing a rather trilly or canary-like effect. The songs begin with 1 to 4 relatively long, steady or slightly down-slurred, whistled notes (or 2-note phrases in which one note is much longer than the other); these introductory notes or phrases are generally of two types, one higher in pitch than the other. The introductory notes are followed by 2 to 7 series of more rapidly uttered phrases; individual songs are usually 2 to 4 seconds in length, and are sung at the rate of about 5 or 6 a minute. The phrase series following the introductory notes may contain up to 10 similar phrases; most of these phrases are uttered slowly enough to be counted. The songs of a given bird usually vary in length—in the number of phrase series and the number of phrases in a series—and in the sequence of the different phrase types; sometimes they may vary in the character of the introductory notes. The songs of different birds usually contain slightly different phrases.

AMERICAN GOLDFINCH
Spinus tristis

The songs of the **American Goldfinch** are twittery and canary-like, and consist of a series of short phrases or trills; sometimes (Example 1) they are short and separated by silent intervals of several seconds, and sometimes (Example 2) the song is long-continued. A characteristic call, usually uttered in flight, is a *per-chick-a-tee* (Example 3), with the *chick* the loudest and highest in pitch, and the *a-tee* lower in pitch.

HOUSE WREN
Troglodytes aedon

House Wren songs consist of 5 to 10 (usually 6 or 8) series of trilly phrases, and might be described as a bubbling chatter. The introductory notes are usually uttered more slowly than the rest and are generally low-pitched; the pitch is highest in about the middle of the song, and usually falls slightly toward the end. Most phrases are 1- or 2-noted, and are uttered too fast to be counted (10 to 20 per second). The songs in this species, in a given bird and in different birds, vary in much the same way as those of the Vesper Sparrow. House Wren songs are generally sung at the rate of 6 to 10 per minute.

BOBOLINK
Dolichonyx oryzivorus

   The songs of the **Bobolink** are similar to those of the preceding species in this track in consisting of several series of similar phrases, but they seldom contain more than two or three similar phrases in succession, and the song's quality is quite distinctive. The songs are rollicking and tinkling, and vary in length; some songs are several seconds in length. The songs may be sung from a perch—usually a weed or fence post—or in flight. Different songs (of the same or different birds) are similar in general character, but vary in length and in the nature of the individual notes and phrases.

The songs in this track are long-continued, and consist of a great variety of phrases. The phrases of a given bird vary greatly in quality; some are clear whistles (usually slurred), some are harsh or nasal, and some contain both clear and harsh elements. All three of the species in this track occasionally include in their songs what appear to be imitations of other birds; this feature is particularly noticeable in the song of the Mockingbird. Each bird of these three species has a vocabulary of a large number of different phrases; these phrases are not sung in any fixed sequence.

CATBIRD
Dumetella carolinensis

The most distinctive feature of the song of the **Catbird*** is the fact that successive phrases are nearly always different; the phrases are not repeated as they are in a Thrasher or Mockingbird: Also, relatively more phrases in this bird's vocabulary are nasal or whining in quality than in the other two species. A common call note, from which the bird gets its name, is a cat-like *meow;* one such note is heard about 11 seconds from the beginning of the example on the CD, and two more are heard in about the middle of the recording.

The song of the **Brown Thrasher** is very similar to that of the Catbird, but the phrases are more or less grouped; most phrase groups contain only 2 or 3 phrases, and these phrases are usually identical or very similar. Perhaps the most distinctive feature of the thrasher's song is the fact that many of its phrases are sung 2 or 3 times in succession; the Catbird seldom sings two similar phrases in succession, and the Mockingbird usually repeats its phrases several times before changing to another phrase.

---

*Gray Catbird.

BROWN THRASHER
Toxostoma rufum

MOCKINGBIRD
Mimus polyglottos

The song of the **Mockingbird*** is very similar to those of the two preceding species, but it is usually somewhat more musical in quality, with fewer harsh notes, and many of its phrases are sung several times in succession before the bird changes to a different phrase. In many phrase series the change in phrase type is rather gradual through the series. The Mockingbird gets its name from its habit of including in its repertoire notes and phrases similar to those of other birds. This mimicking is remarkably accurate in some cases, and it is only by listening to the bird for a little while (sooner or later the Mockingbird will change its phrases) that one can be sure he is listening to a

---

*Northern Mockingbird.

Mockingbird and not to the bird mimicked; we believe this is true mimicry, and not accidental similarity. In other cases the mimicking is not so accurate, and it may be a matter of opinion on the part of the listener whether or not a particular series of phrases represents an imitation of another bird. Northern birds include more mimicry in their singing than southern birds. Example 2 contains relatively good imitations of a Killdeer, a Carolina Wren, and a Kingfisher, and an only fair imitation of a Phoebe; the notes at the end of this recording are very similar to the scolding notes of a Bewick's Wren.

TABLE SHOWING LOCALITY AND MONTH IN WHICH SONGS WERE RECORDED

Where no number is given, the songs or calls are practically continuous; a *c* in song column indicates a recording containing calls.

Species	Example	Songs	Location/Month
TRACK 1			
COMMON CROW	1	5c	Maine/June
Corvus brachyrhynchos	2		Ohio/March
BLUE JAY	1	7c	Florida/March
Cyanocitta cristata	2	12c	N. H./March
	3	7c	Ohio/February
COMMON NICHTHAWK	1	14c	Ohio/May
Chordeiles minor			
HOUSE SPARROW	1	12c	Ohio/April
Passer domesticus			
BOBWHITE	1	5c	Ohio/May
Colinus virginianus			
RED-SHOULDERED HAWK	1		Florida/March
Buteo lineatus			
WHIP-POOR-WILL	1	18c	Ohio/June
Caprimulgus vociferus			
TRACK 2			
BLACK-CAPPED CHICKADEE	1	3	Maine/June
Parus atricapillus	2	3	Maine/August
CAROLINA CHICKADEE	1	2	Ohio/May
Parus carolinensis	2	2	Florida/March
	3	3	Ohio/May
BLACK-CAPPED CHICKADEE	1	4c	Maine/August
Parus atricapillus			
CAROLINA CHICKADEE	1	4c	Ohio/March
Parus carolinensis			

TABLE SHOWING LOCALITY AND MONTH IN WHICH SONGS WERE RECORDED

Species	Example	Songs	Location/Month
EASTERN WOOD PEWEE *Contopus virens*	1	6	Ohio/May
EASTERN PHOEBE *Sayornis phoebe*	1	11	Ohio/April
LEAST FLYCATCHER *Empidonax minimus*	1		Maine/July
GREAT CRESTED FLYCATCHER *Myiarchus crinitus*	1 2	4 3	Ohio/May Ohio/May
TRAILL'S FLYCATCHER *Empidonax traillii*	1 2	5 4	Ohio/May Vermont/June

TRACK 3

Species	Example	Songs	Location/Month
WHITE-BREASTED NUTHATCH *Sitta carolinensis*	1 2	c 5	Ohio/October Ohio/April
YELLOW-SHAFTED FLICKER *Colaptes auratus*	1	4	Ohio/May
CHIPPING SPARROW *Spizella passerina*	1 2 3 4 5 6 7 8	1 1 1 1 1 1 1 1	Maine/June Ohio/May Ohio/May Ohio/May Maine/July N.C./April Ohio/May Michigan/May
SLATE-COLORED JUNCO *Junco hyemalis*	1 2 3 4 5 6 7 8 9	1 1 1 1 1 1 1 1 1	Maine/July Maine/July Maine/June Maine/June Maine/June Maine/July Maine/August Maine/July Michigan/May
SWAMP SPARROW *Melospiza georgiana*	1 2 3 4 5 6 7	1 1 1 1 1 1 1	Maine/June Maine/July Maine/July Ohio/May Ohio/May Maine/July Maine/July

TABLE SHOWING LOCALITY AND MONTH
IN WHICH SONGS WERE RECORDED

Species	Example	Songs	Location/Month
NASHVILLE WARBLER	1	1	Maine/June
Vermivora ruficapilla	2	1	Ohio/May
	3	1	Maine/June
	4	1	Maine/July
	5	1	Ohio/May
	6	1	Ohio/May

TRACK 4

Species	Example	Songs	Location/Month
YELLOWTHROAT	1	1	Ohio/May
Geothlypis trichas	2	1	Maine/July
	3	1	Maine/July
	4	1	Ohio/May
	5	1	Ohio/May
	6	1	Maine/July
	7	1	Maine/June
	8	1	Maine/June
CAROLINA WREN	1	1	Ohio/April
Thryothorus ludovicianus	2	1	Ohio/March
	3	1	Ohio/May
	4	1	Ohio/May
	5	1	Ohio/May
	6	1	Ohio/May
	7	1	Ohio/April
	8	1	Ohio/June
	9	1	Ohio/April
OVENBIRD	1	2	Ohio/May
Seiurus aurocapillus	2	2	Ohio/April
	3	2	Maine/July
KENTUCKY WARBLER	1	2	Ohio/May
Oporornis formosus	2	2	Ohio/May
	3	2	Ohio/May

TRACK 5

Species	Example	Songs	Location/Month
FIELD SPARROW	1	1	Ohio/April
Spizella pusilla	2	1	Ohio/April
	3	1	Ohio/April
	4	1	Ohio/March
	5	1	Ohio/April
	6	1	Ohio/April
WHITE-THROATED SPARROW	1	1	Maine/June
Zonotrichia albicollis	2	1	Maine/June
	3	1	Maine/June
	4	1	Maine/June
	5	1	Ohio/April
	6	1	Maine/July

TABLE SHOWING LOCALITY AND MONTH IN WHICH SONGS WERE RECORDED

Species	Example	Songs	Location/Month
CARDINAL	1	1	Ohio/March
Richmondena cardinalis	2	1	Ohio/April
	3	1	Ohio/March
	4	1	Ohio/April
	5	1	Ohio/March
	6	1	Ohio/May
	7	1	Ohio/March
	8	1	Ohio/April
TUFTED TITMOUSE	1	1	Ohio/May
Parus bicolor	2	1	Ohio/April
	3	1	Florida/April
	4	1	W.Va./April
	5	1	Ohio/April
	6	1	Ohio/April
	7	1	Ohio/April
EASTERN MEADOWLARK	1	3	Ohio/May
Sturnella magna	2	1	Florida/March
	3	2	Ohio/April
	4	1	Florida/March
	5	6c	Ohio/April
BALTIMORE ORIOLE	1	3	Ohio/May
Icterus galbula	2	1	Ohio/May
	3	1	Maine/June
	4	1	Ohio/April
	5	1	Ohio/May
	6	1	Ohio/May

TRACK 6

Species	Example	Songs	Location/Month
GRASSHOPPER SPARROW	1	3	Ohio/May
Ammodramus savannarum	2	3	Ohio/May
BLUE-WINGED WARBLER	1	3	Ohio/May
Vermivora pinus	2	2	Ohio/May
BLACK-THROATED	1	3	Maine/July
GREEN WARBLER	2	2	Maine/June
Dendroica virens	3	1	Maine/June
PRAIRIE WARBLER	1	3	N.C./May
Dendroica discolor	2	2	Ohio/June
PARULA WARBLER	1	2	Maine/June
Parula americana	2	2	Maine/July
	3	2	Maine/June
	4	1	Maine/July
CERULEAN WARBLER	1	1	Ohio/May
Dendroica cerulea	2	1	Ohio/April

TABLE SHOWING LOCALITY AND MONTH IN WHICH SONGS WERE RECORDED

Species	Example	Songs	Location/Month
	3	1	Ohio/May
	4	1	Ohio/May
	5	1	Ohio/May
	6	1	W.Va./May
	7	1	Ohio/May
TRACK 7			
ROBIN	1		Maine/June
Turdus migratorius			
ROSE-BREASTED GROSBEAK	1	1	Maine/June
Pheucticus ludovicianus	2	1	Ohio/May
	3	2	Ohio/May
SUMMER TANAGER	1	2	N.C./May
Piranga rubra	2	3	Ohio/May
SCARLET TANAGER	1	2	Ohio/May
Piranga olivacea	2	3	Ohio/May
RED-EYED VIREO	1		Ohio/May
Vireo olivaceus			
WARBLING VIREO	1	2	Ohio/May
Vireo gilvus	2	2	Ohio/May
PURPLE FINCH	1	2	Maine/July
Carpodacus purpureus	2	2	Maine/June
	3	1	Maine/July
TRACK 8			
WOOD THRUSH	1	8	Ohio/July
Hylocichla mustelina	2	4	Ohio/May
RUFOUS-SIDED TOWHEE	1	1	Ohio/April
Pipilo erythrophthalmus	2	1	Maine/July
	3	1	Maine/July
	4	1	Maine/July
	5	1	N.C./May
	6	1	N.C./May
	7	1	Ohio/March
	8	1	Maine/July
RED-WINGED BLACKBIRD	1	1	Ohio/April
Agelaius phoeniceus	2	1	Ohio/May
	3	1	Ohio/May
	4	1	Ohio/April
	5	1	Ohio/April
	6	1	Florida/March

TABLE SHOWING LOCALITY AND MONTH IN WHICH SONGS WERE RECORDED

Species	Example	Songs	Location/Month
SONG SPARROW	1	1	Ohio/May
Melospiza melodia	2	1	Ohio/March
	3	1	Maine/August
	4	1	Maine/July
	5	1	Maine/July
	6	1	Maine/July
	7	1	Ohio/March
	8	1	Maine/June
	9	1	Maine/July
HOODED WARBLER	1	2	N.C./April
Wilsonia citrina	2	1	Ohio/May
	3	1	Ohio/May
	4	2	Ohio/May
YELLOW WARBLER	1	1	Maine/June
Dendroica petechia aestiva	2	1	Ohio/May
	3	1	Maine/July
	4	1	Maine/June
	5	1	Maine/June
	6	1	Maine/June
	7	1	Maine/June
CHESTNUT-SIDED WARBLER	1	1	Maine/July
Dendroica pensylvanica	2	1	Maine/July
	3	1	Maine/July
	4	1	Ohio/May
	5	1	Ohio/May
	6	1	Ohio/May
	7	1	Ohio/May
WHITE-EYED VIREO	1	1	Ohio/May
Vireo griseus	2	1	Ohio/June
	3	4	Ohio/May
	4	1	Florida/April
	5	1	Florida/March

TRACK 9

Species	Example	Songs	Location/Month
LOUISIANA WATERTHRUSH	1	2	Ohio/May
Seiurus motacilla	2	2	Ohio/May
	3	2	Ohio/April
INDIGO BUNTING	1	2	Ohio/May
Passerina cyanea	2	1	Maine/July
	3	1	Ohio/May
	4	2	Ohio/May
VESPER SPARROW	1	1	Ohio/April
Pooecetes gramineus	2	1	Ohio/April

TABLE SHOWING LOCALITY AND MONTH
IN WHICH SONGS WERE RECORDED

Species	Example	Songs	Location/Month
	3	1	Ohio/April
	4	1	Ohio/May
	5	1	Ohio/May
	6	1	Ohio/May
AMERICAN GOLDFINCH	1	3	Maine/July
Spinus tristis	2		Ohio/May
	3	8c	Ohio/May
HOUSE WREN	1	1	Ohio/May
Troglodytes aedon	2	1	Ohio/May
	3	1	Ohio/May
	4	1	Ohio/May
	5	1	Ohio/July
	6	1	Ohio/May
BOBOLINK	1	6	Ohio/May
Dolichonyx oryzivorus			

TRACK 10

Species	Example	Songs	Location/Month
CATBIRD	1		Ohio/May
Dumetella carolinensis			
BROWN THRASHER	1		Ohio/May
Toxostoma rufum			
MOCKINGBIRD	1		Florida/March
Mimus polyglottos	2		Ohio/April

SPECTROGRAPHS

The figures consist of sound spectrographs of bird songs, prepared from tape recordings by means of a Vibralyzer sound
spectrograph. All graphs are of songs on the CD. Frequencies
are shown in kilocycles per second rather than in terms of the
notes of our musical scale; 4 kilocycles per second is approxi-
mately the pitch of the top note of a piano, and 2 kilocycles per
second is an octave lower. References to the songs on the CD
refer to the songs of the species concerned.

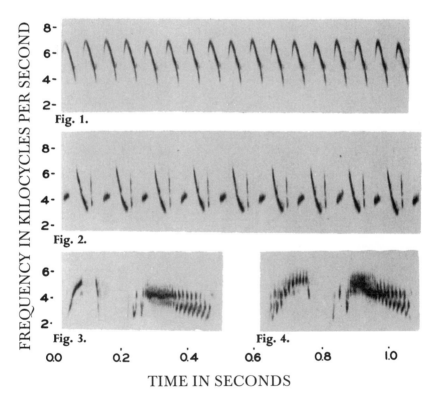

Fig. 1. Chipping Sparrow, about one second of the seventh song.
Fig. 2. Swamp Sparrow, about one second of the seventh song.
Fig. 3. Traill's Flycatcher, a *fitz-bew* song, the first song.
Fig. 4. Traill's Flycatcher, a *fizz-bew* song, the second song.

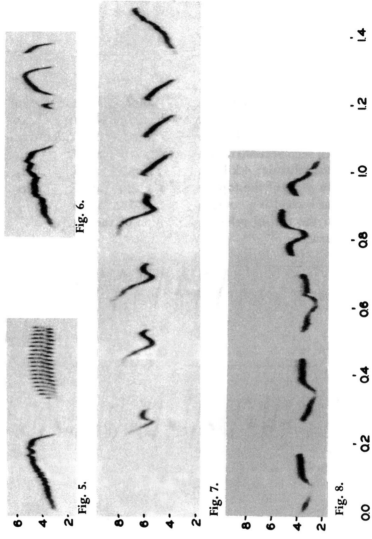

FREQUENCY IN KILOCYCLES PER SECOND

Fig. 5. Eastern Phoebe, a song ending in a buzz, the second song.
Fig. 6. Eastern Phoebe, a song ending in a sputter, the third song.
Fig. 7. Yellow Warbler, the third song on the CD.
Fig. 8. Hooded Warbler, the first song on the CD.
Fig. 9. Cerulean Warbler, the fourth song on the CD.
Fig. 10. Chestnut-sided Warbler, the first song on the CD.
Fig. 11. Louisiana Waterthrush, the first song on the CD.

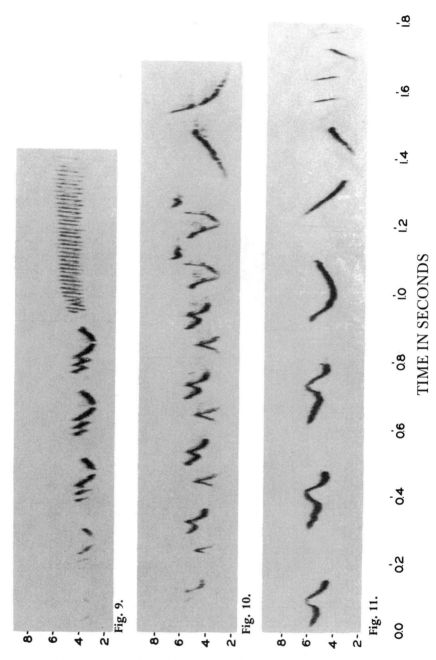

Fig. 9.

Fig. 10.

Fig. 11.

FREQUENCY IN KILOCYCLES PER SECOND

TIME IN SECONDS

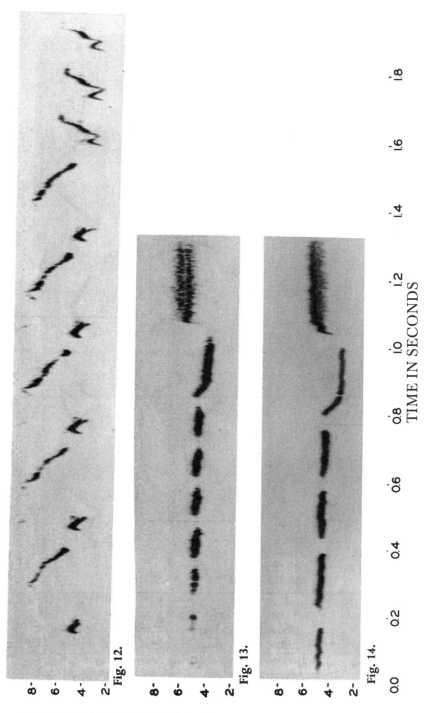

Fig. 12.

Fig. 13.

Fig. 14.

FREQUENCY IN KILOCYCLES PER SECOND

TIME IN SECONDS

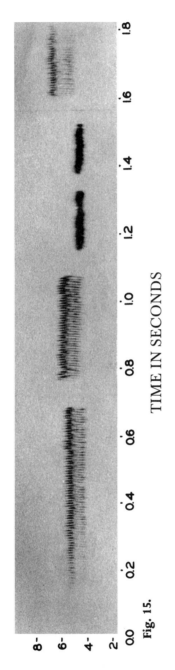

TIME IN SECONDS

Fig. 15.

Fig. 12. Nashville Warbler, the second song on the CD.
Fig. 13–15. Black-throated Green Warbler.
    Fig. 13. The sixth song on the CD (Example 3).
    Fig. 14. The fourth song on the CD (Example 2).
    Fig. 15. The third song on the CD (Example 1).